ISBN 1-85717-047-4

9 781857 170474

KT-492-955

GETTING RESULTS
Unlocking Community Care
in Partnership with
Disabled People

Barrie Fiedler

Partnership Paper No 1

Published by the King's Fund Centre
126 Albert Street
London
NW1 7NF
Tel: 071-267 6111

© Living Options Partnership 1993

ISBN 1 85717 047 4

A CIP catalogue record for this book is available from the British Library

Distributed by Bournemouth English Book Centre (BEBC)
PO Box 1496
Poole
Dorset
BH12 3YD

The Living Options Partnership is a collaborative venture between The Prince of Wales' Advisory Group on Disability and the King's Fund Centre, with additional funding from the Department of Health.

The Prince of Wales' Advisory Group on Disability exists to assist HRH The Prince of Wales in unifying perspectives and acting as a catalyst to enhance the values, attitudes and practices of society as they relate to disability.

The King's Fund Centre is a service development agency which promotes improvements in health and social care. We do this by working with people in health and social services, in voluntary agencies, and with the users of these services. We encourage people to try out new ideas, provide financial or practical support to new developments, and enable experiences to be shared through workshops, conferences, information services and publications. Our aim is to ensure that good developments in health and social care are widely taken up. The King's Fund Centre is part of the King's Fund.

CONTENTS

Foreword

At a time of vital significance in the strategic development of community care service provision, we commend this study, which describes a wide range of good practice. The fundamental key to valued provision is whether disabled people have been involved in the planning, providing and monitoring of services.

The context of the innovative approaches and projects contained within the document is one of a plethora of conflicting demands, particularly in relation to financial and professional guidelines. The schemes highlighted have been achieved in the face of a discouraging array of obstacles and represent just a few bright spots in a generally bleak picture of disability services nationally.

The continued goodwill and participation of disabled people cannot reasonably be expected in a climate that is not conducive to positive change. We call on all those in positions of responsibility, at all levels, to ensure that the community care enterprise moves beyond consultative processes and produces real services that give users the quality of life and personal autonomy they seek.

Barbara Stocking
Director
King's Fund Centre

Peter Holland
Co-ordinator
The Prince of Wales' Advisory Group
on Disability

 iv

Summary

Statutory and voluntary agencies and disabled people throughout the country are working to meet the challenge of providing effective community care. Since 1985 Living Options has supported the development of responsive services for people with physical and sensory disabilities. This paper draws on the experiences of a number of localities, including the Living Options Practice Localities, to demonstrate how responsive services are being achieved and to suggest key factors that produce results.

Getting Results began with a trawl for positive changes – quality services, increased user control, effective partnerships – resulting from new ways of working in the spirit of community care. The response to the trawl shows, however, that as the Government's community care programme comes into effect, services in most localities and for most disabled people remain inappropriate, insufficient, inflexible, fragmented and poorly resourced. Among the findings:

- Physical and sensory disability services are in danger of returning to low priority status, despite a heightened profile over the past few years. Physical disability is likely to become a 'bolt-on' to services for elderly people, on whom much community care-related activity is focused.

- Service planning and user involvement in the planning process have become ends in themselves and dominate authorities' agendas at the expense of service development. This planning 'industry' demands endless time and energy in committees and meetings, with little to show for the effort.

- Lack of money is causing concern everywhere. While there is scope for redistribution of resources, budget restrictions are resulting in cuts in practical services for disabled people, loss of funds for voluntary organisations providing good support services, and limited resources for new initiatives.

- Professionals and users describe an obstacle course of new systems, traditional attitudes and lack of resources which must be overcome or side-stepped in order to achieve even small successes. Restructuring of health and social services has created new complications and delays.

- Good practice is most evident where disabled people are active. The expertise and commitment offered (and challenges posed) by disabled people's groups are valued by authorities with a tradition of partnership working; but such groups, and the services they provide, are marginalised in most localities.

● Few disability services reflect or meet Black disabled people's needs, but few authorities have explored new tactics for reaching minority ethnic communities. Small, quality voluntary projects supporting Black disabled people are rarely acknowledged or funded by authorities.

● Authorities expect understanding and co-operation from disabled people, but often withhold information because of concerns about demands on stretched services, legal action or confidentiality. Failure to share with disabled people issues and implications of policy and funding makes partnership impossible.

● Knowledge about disabled people's needs relies heavily on user representation in the planning process. There is little evidence that information learned through assessment/care management mechanisms is fed into the planning system.

Keys to solutions

Despite these sobering trends, this study did produce evidence of innovative approaches and successful new service developments. Examples of good practice from a number of localities are cited. Based on this evidence, *Getting Results* outlines some keys to unlocking responsive community care services for disabled people. These are grouped according to two broad themes, or 'rings':

● **Purpose**, including clear, shared intentions and targets for services and for user participation; and

● **Strategy**, or the structures and tools required to deliver results.

These keys will be familiar to many localities; failure to use them to open doors will be equally familiar. If community care is to be a success, radical change and acceleration of progress will be needed everywhere. *Getting Results* aims to encourage localities to persevere in developing services in full partnership with disabled people by showing how quality services and greater user control are being achieved in some localities and what the benefits are to those involved.

Introduction

Context

The Government's community care reforms aim to enable individuals to live independently with co-ordinated support in the community and to have a greater say about the services they use. The NHS and Community Care Act 1990 and practice guidance require local authority social service departments to consult with organisations representing users and carers, and with health, housing and other voluntary agencies, about service planning. The involvement of users is emphasised in the assessment of individual need and design of care packages.

For those with an interest in developing effective disability services the reforms offer exciting opportunities, but they also bring frustrations. In the lead-up to full implementation of community care, contributors to this study spoke of raised expectations, organisational turmoil and inadequate resources (see Summary, page v). Despite numerous reports documenting services shortfalls, years of pressure from organisations of disabled people and wide acknowledgement of the need for change, there are still more problems than examples of good practice to share.

Living Options

Since 1985 a series of Living Options projects has worked to empower disabled people and encourage the development of quality services that meet the needs of all disabled people in the community (see Living Options Partnership, page 27). Between 1989 and 1992 Living Options In Practice worked with multi-agency teams and disabled people in eight Practice Localities to foster user participation and build comprehensive disability service systems. This work was documented in project newsletters; three project papers expanded ideas about developing services, involving users and tracking success (see References, page 12). The fundamental themes of the Living Options work – services that respond to disabled people's needs, genuine user participation in service planning and co-ordinated multi-agency working – are also central to community care.

Aims

Against this background, *Getting Results* aims to demonstrate to those planning, commissioning and providing disability services the benefits of responsive community care planning. It cites examples of positive approaches that are achieving quality services, increased user control, effective partnerships and better use of limited resources. Based on this evidence from the field, some essential keys to success are suggested under two themes: a sense of purpose shared by all those involved and the strategy required to bring about positive change.

Getting Results describes how agencies – working together and with disabled people – are actually making things happen. It is not a compendium of 'one-off' good services achieved by chance or individual perseverance or a survey of good ideas and promising plans for services that may be achieved. *Getting Results* documents real accomplishments, achieved through processes that can be repeated, and highlights key elements that help turn theory into practice.

Method

The lessons of this paper are based on two chief sources:
(i) informal discussions between September and December 1992 with social and health service planners, managers and users from about 25 localities in England and Wales and
(ii) work with the eight Practice Teams and user groups involved in the Living Options in Practice project between 1989 and 1992.

Examples described are from localities with and without previous Living Options involvement and at different levels of development, including those starting from a poor service base and with minimal user participation and others that are 'market leaders'. Each example shows *a* way, not *the* way, to achieve good practice.

The achievements of these localities are not necessarily unique nor 'the best' (and no claims were made to that), but their experiences are typical of many localities working to develop effective services. Readers of this paper may have examples of good practice they would like to share, and the Living Options Partnership would like to hear from you. New information about successes in providing effective community care services will be shared in future through the Living Options database and *Network* newsletters.

Definitions

Disabled people/users: physically disabled users or potential users of services. The Living Options work has targeted people aged 16 to 64 with severe physical or sensory disabilities who need long-term support services in order to live in the community.

Carers: relatives or friends helping disabled people living at home. Carers are also users of services, and their needs may be different from disabled people's needs; however, getting services right for disabled people will also benefit carers.

Professionals: paid or volunteer workers in statutory, voluntary or independent agencies that plan, purchase or provide services.

Locality: a geographical 'patch' for service planning and provision which may coincide with a local authority area or health district or may overlap local/district/health authority boundaries. The term 'locality' is used to underline the fact that responsiblity for community care services does not lie entirely with local authorities.

Joint commissioning/partnership/planning team: a group which includes membership from the local authority, health authority, family health services authority and voluntary sector. Such groups are being set up under a variety of names and have responsibility for planning, assessing and purchasing community care services.

Black people: people of African-Caribbean, Asian or other minority ethnic origin.

Keys to getting results

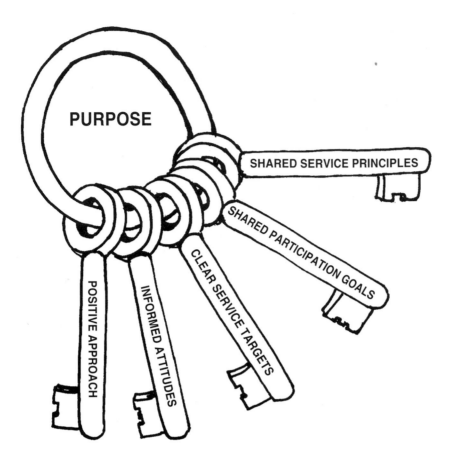

Unlocking community care

- **Shared service principles** based on disabled people's definitions of their needs and concerns

- **Shared participation goals** to increase users' role in service development

- **Clear service targets** to clarify community care aims

- **Informed attitudes** through continuing education and training

- **Positive approach** that turns principles into practice

Unlocking community care

Based on evidence from the field gathered for this study, a number of keys are suggested that will help unlock responsive community care services for disabled people. Two 'rings' of keys are proposed: Section 1, 'Purpose' (see diagram page 4), outlines the attitudes and approaches that will create an environment from which quality services can emerge; Section 2, 'Strategy' (see diagram page 15), suggests structures and techniques for achieving these aims.

Each 'key' is supported by examples from a selection of localities or by reference to earlier Living Options work, offering encouraging evidence of progress (although each example represents a great deal of hard work to overcome barriers, see 'Context', page 1). These examples illustrate how disabled people are playing a vital role in developing community care, how that contribution is valued by the authorities with whom they work, and how tangible results are being achieved in terms of responsive, user-controlled services.

Section 1: Purpose

Responsive community care begins with clear intentions and objectives for achieving effective services shared by everyone with an interest in the outcome: disabled people, planners and commissioners, statutory and voluntary sector providers, senior managers and staff, members of authorities – and the community.

Shared service principles

The principles set out in *Living Options Guidelines*[1], published by The Prince of Wales' Advisory Group on Disability in 1985, place the disabled person firmly at the centre of service planning:

● Choice as to where to live and how to maintain independence without over-protection, or the risk of unnecessary hazards, including help in learning how to choose

● Consultation with disabled people and their families on services as they are planned

● Information clearly presented and readily available to all disabled consumers

- Participation in the life of local and national communities in respect of both responsibilities and benefits

- Recognition that long-term disability is not synonymous with illness and that the medical model of care is usually inappropriate

- Autonomy – that is, freedom to make decisions regarding the way of life best suited to an individual disabled person's circumstances.

Many community care plans and other statutory and voluntary agency policy documents incorporate these principles, which provide a vital underpinning to 'needs-led' community care. The eight Living Options Practice Teams also produced mission statements to qualify further this value base (see Reference 2, page 12).

Shared participation goals

Genuine involvement of disabled people is fundamental to the Living Options approach to service development. *Tracking Success*[2], published in 1991, gives user participation in service planning as a key tracking standard, stating that 'disabled people should have real power over the way services and policies are planned and implemented'. Professionals and users often have different expectations of what 'consultation' and 'participation' in service development entail. All those involved need to recognise disabled people as a vital resource and to be clear about why, when and how they will be involved in planning, designing, providing and monitoring both community and individual services.

Achieving User Participation[3] (1992) sets out some key steps in the process of developing effective participation: reaching consensus about what participation means, funding and supporting effective involvement, establishing user groups and working with disabled people and their organisations as equal partners. It describes a continuum of user participation encompassing information provision, consultation, partnership and delegated control.

Embarking on user participation raises concerns: among professionals, about the prospect of users' anger and demands, and slowing of the planning process; among disabled people, about privacy, control, tokenism. Until each recognises and respects the other's viewpoint, joint working will not occur.

Issues often arise concerning 'representation' of disabled people: how to ensure that representatives speak for a wide spectrum of service users; how to avoid tokenism; how to enable the most marginalised people to become involved. Higher standards of representation are sometimes demanded from disabled people than from professionals or from other client groups such as carers. A single user viewpoint is expected although users themselves legitimately disagree. The same individual may be expected to speak for users on every group, pilot project or committee. Claims to the user voice by organisations run by non-disabled people or carers' groups may cause tensions. Ideally, a collective view will be given via elected members of a broadly-based organisation of disabled people.

Alternative strategies need to be created to involve Black disabled people, who are excluded from traditional planning processes, and for whom services are particularly unresponsive. More effective ways of including deaf and blind people, and people from rural areas, in service development also need to be explored. Of course some people will always choose not to get involved.

Well-organised and informed collective user action helps overcome obstacles to effective participation in community care planning. The longer the history of working with disabled people's groups in a locality, the greater the evidence of benefit. Localities with experience of working with disabled people are confident of the 'payoff' for everyone: effective user involvement enables authorities to meet legislative requirements, gives purpose and weight to their plans and policies (including bids for resources) and leads to services that disabled people want to use.

The continuous challenge posed by a strong and confident collective user voice is welcomed by such localities. A clear strategy for user participation, owned by users and professionals, can turn community care service planning, even in difficult circumstances, into a shared process of critical decision-making rather than a hostile battle about rationing resources and disempowering individuals.

All of the Living Options Practice Teams embarked on user participation strategies, based on the development of disabled people's groups, to suit particular local circumstances. The Living Options newsletters and project papers describe some of this work; a contact for each Practice Locality can be obtained from the Partnership office. Pages 13-14 describe a variety of approaches to involving disabled people in service planning.

Clear service targets

Statements of philosophy are, of course, not enough. Clear objectives for service provision must follow a commitment to principle. Targets must be agreed between professionals and disabled people, incorporated within community care plans, and reviewed regularly.

The Living Options In Practice *Framework for Action*[1] (1990) sets out the essential elements encompassed by any comprehensive service system:

● a response point to users' needs

● a place to live

● personal support services

● access to the community

● specialist services

● opportunities for personal development.

A number of authorities find that this framework is a useful basis for community care planning and have established 'task groups' to tackle each service element.

It is essential that principles and plans result in tangible change for users and providers of services. Many localities point to the importance of ensuring frequent real, if small, successes. Given the pervasive scepticism about the capability or willingness of 'the system' to deliver, and the long lead times for community care planning, everyone needs to see that new ways of working can deliver the goods. Professionals and users must work together to evaluate results: a reorganised service that suits providers may not work better for users.

Measurable, timetabled and achievable targets need to be included in community care plans, and simple, routine tests for progress instituted. Few authorities' first plans, however, go beyond general policy statements, and monitoring of results is only beginning to be addressed in most localities. Disabled people must be involved in monitoring as well as setting service goals. Living Options In Practice's *Tracking Success*[2] (1991) sets out essential criteria for judging user satisfaction, participation and partnership, and suggests ways to obtain feedback from users and staff in order to test results against standards and targets.

The following examples show how disabled people are involved in producing and reviewing community care strategies in four localities.

● **Kingston upon Thames' community care plan sets action plans for each client group. This year's plan for physical and sensory disability was based on activities undertaken by the local authority, the Kingston Association of Disabled People and other groups, as well as on a services strategy produced by the Joint Commissioning Advisory Group (JCAG). User representatives were involved from the start, and their ideas were taken on board. A Community Care Plan Steering Group, which includes four user representatives as well as social services, health, family health services authority and housing, meets monthly to produce and review the plan. JCAG also reviews these targets regularly.**

● **Through the Community Care Forum of voluntary organisations, a number of 'special interest' groups are being set up to work with Hillingdon's Joint Commissioning Group (JCG) on the community care plan. The Disablement Association Hillingdon (DASH), a member – through the Council for Voluntary Service – of the JCG with full voting rights, is organising a group of disabled people based at a local day centre in order to extend consultation beyond its own membership.**

● **A long period of consultation enabled the Waltham Forest Association of Disabled People (WFAPD) and other groups to contribute, through informal meetings as well as through a formal written process, to particular aspects of the community care plan. As a result, the plan's objectives were made more concrete, specifying tasks, budget impact and target completion date for each objective. A new section on Black populations was added, after representation from WFAPD, Black disabled people's organisations and Black community groups, to provide funding for organisations of Asian and African-Caribbean disabled people, outreach work, more sensitive assessment procedures, and more Asian home helps.**

● **In Maidstone, the community care plan for physical and sensory disability is being drafted by the Living Options Practice Team. The Team has delegated this task to four user groups structured around core services: day opportunities, accommodation, respite care and domiciliary care. This will feed directly into the Area Joint Planning Group.**

Informed attitudes

Views about service provision and user involvement must be challenged continually through education and training programmes. Understanding has grown, particularly among managers and officers who play a lead role in disability services, many of whom have had 'disability equality' training. Such training should not be seen as an end in itself, however, but as the beginning of a process of change. Professionals and users need to check their perceptions of attitudes: the former may report a cultural 'sea change' in their agencies, while the latter may see little or no change.

Education and training are needed to extend this understanding and commitment to staff at all levels, and to members of authorities who have a new and more complex role to play in community care planning and resourcing. Joint training, and training of professionals by disabled people, help build effective joint working. Awareness must be so engrained in 'the system' that good practice will not depend on the perseverence of committed individuals.

The use of language is important. Terms such as 'purchaser', 'quality assurance', and 'outcome' mean little to most people. Those writing about community care should avoid jargon and use language that lay people understand.

Changing attitudes about disability services can be achieved in a variety of ways:

● **A work programme for forty to fifty severely disabled people and an advocacy service for people with multiple disabilities are among the achievements of an initiative begun in Hillingdon in 1991. 'Principles into Practice' brought together users, parents, carers and social services staff to consider the daytime service needs of disabled people. Issues included jobs, empowerment and advocacy, and involved sometimes painful discussions about competing agendas of different people involved. 'Principles into Practice' evolved from an earlier exercise during which an independently facilitated group of users and staff of social services aimed to establish 'touchstones' and 'outcomes' for social services. This exercise highlighted the importance of listening to one another, and the need for sufficient time and space to consult effectively.**

- **The Wirral Living Options user group is establishing a reputation for training on disability issues both locally and regionally. Disabled people have attended courses to increase their expertise and are now working with the regional health authority, Wirral Hospitals Trust and social services as well as with neighbouring authorities and voluntary organisations.**

- **Disabled people in Hampshire are routinely invited to attend joint social services training courses for managers and officers on advocacy, interviewing and selection, and communication skills. To meet demand disabled people are running additional courses which social services staff are invited to attend.**

- **The expenditure of £5000 has been agreed to by the Redbridge Community Care Planning Team for a two-year programme of training, by disabled people involved with Living Options, of senior managers in the statutory services, with the intention of 'cascading' this training down through the authorities.**

- **Ethnic monitoring since June 1992 is revealing how use of services reflects Black populations in Brent. This exercise, carried out by Parkside Health Trust, is likely to result in the commissioning of race and disability awareness training. Black disabled people's groups are involved in joint training with statutory authorities, and translation of agency documents into minority languages is also underway.**

Positive approach

Results flow from a commitment not only to shared aims and objectives but also from a belief that philosophies and plans can make a real difference, and from a will to make things happen. There is a marked difference between the performance, as well as the atmosphere, of those 'can-do' localities where all those involved believe they can change things despite hard times, and those where the prevailing attitude is one of defeat. A positive approach reflects not only individual attitudes but also a political framework that encourages innovation and action.

Understanding others' viewpoints, learning to work together and getting results takes time and experience. Local authorities working to community care deadlines imposed by Government are concerned about commissioning, contracting for private care, assessment procedures and care management. Disabled people are looking for real changes in housing, personal assistance, counselling, jobs and transport. The pressure of meeting deadlines (for example, key tasks set by the Community Care Support Force) must not result in traditional solutions (reorganisation of services provided in traditional ways) at the expense of more innovative responses (for example, self-organised personal assistance schemes). Decisions need to be made now on the best information available, but solutions must ensure continuing discussion and the possibility of change.

Funding for community care remains uncertain, and the amount available for physical disablity services is less clear still. Public expenditure controls and social security transfer arrangements mean real cuts in services are likely. Adequate funds are clearly essential but there is still scope for change and improvement – by shifting major resourcing of inappropriate services (for example, from day 'centres' to mainstream education or employment opportunities, or from residential care to home-based personal assistance schemes); and by giving disabled people control over decisions about their lives (for example, through a more active role in the assessment and care management process).

Creative localities can make progress in the midst of (and even take advantage of) the turmoil in planning systems. But they must work towards a future in which services are delivered because of, not in spite of, the system.

The examples on pages 13-14 show how services are being changed through user involvement.

References

1. *Living Options Guidelines for those Planning Services for People with Severe Physical Disabilities.* The Prince of Wales' Advisory Group on Disability. London, 1985. Out of print.

2. *Tracking Success: Testing services for people with severe physical and sensory disabilities.* Fiedler B. Living Options In Practice. London, 1991.

3. *Achieving Using Participation: Planning services for people with severe physical and sensory disabilities.* Fiedler B, Twitchin D. Living Options In Practice. London, 1992.

4. *A Framework For Action: Developing services for people with severe physical and sensory disabilities.* Fiedler B, Twitchin D. Living Options In Practice. London, 1990.

Changing services in partnership with disabled people

- A new 'mobile' resource service in Gloucestershire, supplementing a 'building'-based resource centre, was agreed on after involvement of disabled people through the joint planning process. A resource centre was proposed by a group of professionals based on a survey in 1986, but the proposal was shelved during the period of restructuring of the joint planning process. With support from a newly appointed consumer care organiser, the proposal was re-tested through consumer groups. Disabled people from rural areas of the county, led by the Cheltenham Monitor users' group, were unhappy with a building-based service and agreed to redraft the proposal. The new plan, calling for a small independent living centre in Gloucester and a flexible mobile service for rural areas, was agreed on and a joint finance bid approved. An occupational therapist has just been appointed to put the service into effect.

- A proposal for a sitting service in North Staffordshire was abandoned in favour of a Crossroads scheme after consultation with users. The Disability Planning Forum was considering a sitting service but found little interest among disabled people, who favoured a Crossroads-type service. The planning group agreed to support a Crossroads scheme, which previously had been refused funding in the area.

- A Disabled Persons Accommodation Agency, managed in association with Living Options in Maidstone, will match disabled people with suitable housing throughout Kent. Accommodation for rent or sale will be sought from all sectors including district councils, estate agents and housing associations. Information about vacancies and waiting lists will contribute to future housing strategies across the county. The project is being developed and staffed by disabled people, and funding is expected shortly.

- A number of disabled people who attend a Disability Resource Centre in Waltham Forest meet with social service occupational therapists in a Quality Circle to discuss assessment for and use of aids and equipment. This provides an opportunity to evaluate the service, identifying its strengths and weaknesses. Two years on, following initial training, a self-selected core group of users maintains this quality monitoring process, and also comments on other assessment forms to be used widely in community care implementation.

- A social services day centre in Hampshire was scheduled for replacement until discussions were opened with the local community. Substantial funding goes to the centre which is used by 82 disabled people, while many more in the district are looking for a different kind of service or are too far away for access. A Basingstoke Task Group for Disability Services was convened including social services officers and Basingstoke Users Group members. The different views of local disabled people – some working to retain the centre, some wanting a different kind of 'centre', and others wanting a different dispersal of funds – are being discussed and negotiated in the search for a solution.

- Following discussions by the Wirral Living Options Practice Team (which includes ten service users), a Housing and Disabled People's Group has been established with the Wirral Borough Council Housing Department with a brief to produce a position statement and promote a strategy for improving the provision of accessible housing in the public and private sectors.

- A health plan is being produced in Northampton as required by Oxfordshire Regional Health Authority's 'Toward 2000' initiative. The DHA agreed that the Living Options Group should write the health plan for disabled people. A member of the Living Options Group was selected to lead a working team on each of 11 'health gain' areas identified. To ensure user input to each gain area, topic groups – facilitated by disabled co-ordinators and funded by joint finance – are being set up across the county. Group members are drawn from a consumer database which enables the selection of disabled people with knowledge of and interest in particular issues. 'Health gain' areas now under discussion include the needs of young disabled people leaving full time education.

Keys to getting results

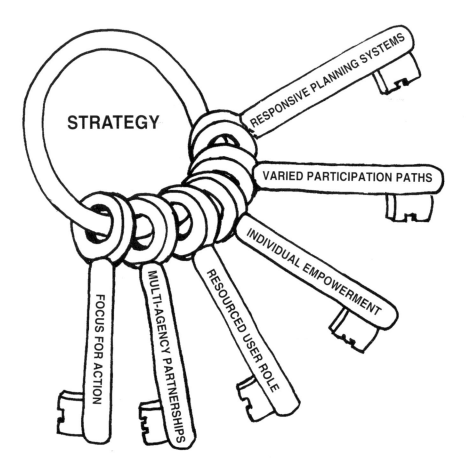

Unlocking community care

- **Responsive planning systems** to ensure users' active involvement in decision-making

- **Varied participation paths** for a wide spectrum of user views

- **Individual empowerment** to enable all disabled people to contribute and effect change

- **Resourced user role** to acknowledge and strengthen the contribution of disabled people and their groups

- **Multi-agency partnerships** to secure seamless community care services

- **Focus for action** to lead and co ordinate service development

Section 2: Strategy

Responsive community care requires that structures are in place through which principles and goals can be met. All those involved need to understand how these mechanisms operate to increase disabled people's control and to deliver quality services.

Responsive planning systems

New community care planning and implementation systems must be straightforward and accessible, preserve the strengths of old structures where successful, ensure active user involvement in decision-making and provide continuity during times of change.

Restructuring of joint planning systems and reorganisation within health and local authorities continues to produce confusion and concern among users and professionals. There is evidence that good practice in joint working between agencies and with disabled people, achieved through hard work and experience, is being lost as new community care planning systems replace, bypass or duplicate existing systems. The confusion may be compounded by parallel 'consultation' systems: for example, a joint commissioning team consults with a new community care forum about service priorities, while at the same time a joint planning team consults an existing disability group about joint finance bids.

In order to have a significant influence over planning and resourcing of services, disabled people and disability teams need access to decision-making at senior levels. Planning teams where users have direct face-to-face contact with decision-makers have been powerful. In some localities disabled people fear exclusion from new community care planning/commissioning teams.

The examples below describe new planning systems that are responsive to users' views.

● **A Joint Commissioning Advisory Group (JCAG) for each client group in Kingston upon Thames represents the local and health authority, family health service authority (FHSA), voluntary sector, users and carers. Membership of the disability JCAG includes a representative from Kingston Association of Disabled People (KADP), through Kingston Council of Voluntary Service (KCVS), one service user and one carer. The JCAG reports to a Joint Commissioning Board of chief executives and chairs of JCAGs. A KCVS officer has a remit to ensure that each JCAG has**

democratically chosen user, carer and voluntary sector representatives.

- Social Care Planning Groups (SCPG) cover the four divisions of the County of Dyfed. The SCPG is a joint group including social services, health, FHSA and voluntary sector representatives. A Task Group for physical disability comprises approximately 50 per cent of its members from the statutory services, and 50 per cent from users, carers and voluntary bodies. Social services are currently drawing up with users and carers a strategy for the department on user/carer participation for all client groups.

- Membership of the Joint Implementation Group (JIG) in Brent reflects the substantial Black population in the locality, including representation from the Asian People with Disabilities Alliance (ADPA) and the Brent Black Disabled People's Association (BBDPA), as well as from social services, health providers, FHSA, community health council and Brent Association of Disabled People (BADP). Joint finance monies to promote user empowerment pay expenses of representatives from groups such as BADP, ADPA and BBDPA.

- The Joint Partnership Group for physical and sensory disability in Northallerton comprises 12 members from social services, health (purchaser and provider), district council (including housing), FHSA, a voluntary aid co-ordinator, and user and carer representatives. User membership includes the Living Options development worker who represents three local Living Options user groups.

- In Hampshire, budgets and responsibility for services are entirely devolved to 17 social services areas. Through local social services user groups, disabled people are increasingly involved in decision making. Core funding to support user participation comes from social services area budgets, with top up from health and other agencies.

Disabled people's views need to reach local authority members and member-level strategy groups, too.

- Disabled people's groups are represented on Waltham Forest Borough Council committees, including the social services and the disability equality committees.

- An advisory representative from the Kingston Association of Disabled People (KADP) sits on the social services committee, and the chair of the social services committee sits on KADP's Executive. KADP is invited to comment on all social services committee agendas.

Varied participation paths

There is a variety of ways through which disabled people can have an impact on service planning and development. A process by which disabled people elect representatives from their formally constituted membership organisations should be a long term goal in every locality, but the development of groups and processes takes time, support and funds, and the absence of a 'perfect' system must not be an excuse to ignore the available user contribution. It is important that localities start where they are, with the 'user voice' as they find it, while resourcing and supporting disabled people and their organisations, from all population groups, to build constituencies, improve representative structures, develop committee skills and gain confidence.

The following are just some of the possible ways that disabled people can be involved. Authorities will want to encourage the use of all these options to draw on the widest base of local experience.

- *Members of formally constituted organisations of disabled people represent their constituency on planning or advisory groups.* **Examples of representative user organisations – Asian People With Disabilities Alliance (Brent), Kingston Association of Disabled People, Disablement Association Hillingdon, Waltham Forest Association of Disabled People – are given elsewhere in this paper. In Hampshire, a county-wide Social Services Consumer Group (SSCG) includes elected representatives from key service areas: day centres, residential homes, Self Operated Care Scheme (SOCS) and care attendant schemes. SSCG considers policy issues, users' grievances, information provision and training. Local groups focus on particular issues: for example, the Hampshire Centre for Independent Living is funded by social services to support and train users and professionals regarding SOCS and other aspects of support/care in independent living. Participation by disabled people is seen as so successful that social services plan to extend the approach to other client groups through a Hampshire Users' Bureau.**

- *Disabled people give their views through informal groups.* In Redbridge, two members of the Deaf Group and two members of the Visual Impairment Liaison Group are participants on the Physical and Sensory Disability Sub-group of the Community Care Planning Group (and one member of the Deaf Group has recently been elected to the Joint Consultative Committee).

  In Hillingdon the Disablement Association (DASH) is increasingly taking on an umbrella co-ordinating role, working with 'special interest' disability groups convened to provide advice to the statutory authorities on particular issues.

- *Disability forums are linked to the formal planning structure.* The Northallerton Practice Team had problems involving disabled people in a rural area with little history of consumer involvement. User groups in three local communities were organised by the Living Options development worker, who sits on the Joint Partnership Group. Although the user groups include only a small number of disabled people, they contribute greater experience and knowledge of issues than previously available in Northallerton. Work will continue to develop wider involvement and more local user groups.

  In East Devon, the Living Options Working Party comprises local groups of and for disabled people as well as individuals, broadly mirroring the national working party. It is regarded as the consultative body by the statutory agencies, undertaking joint work with them and commissioning studies on issues such as housing, domiciliary support and wheelchair provision. The Working Party sends three representatives to the Joint Planning Forum which directly feeds the district's Joint Purchaser Group.

- *Disabled people contribute in an individual capacity through public meetings, committees and topic groups.* In Northampton two disabled co-ordinators bring together interested individuals, via a consumer data base of 1400 disabled people across the county, in 'topic groups' which consider plans/issues raised by the statutory authorities.

- *Individuals react to particular services through the complaints procedure.* An independent Complaints Panel in Kingston includes users (via the Kingston Association of Disabled People) and carers but no social services members. KADP mediate on behalf of complainants.

- *Disabled people lobby decision-makers through campaigning organisations and public demonstrations.* In Maidstone the Disabled Person's Liaison Committee lobbied for access to a newly constructed leisure centre, and gained support from the Living Options Practice Team and the borough council through the committee structure.

- *Information is aggregated on individuals' needs and experiences, via the assessment and care management process and practitioner work loads.* New approaches to needs assessment, including self-assessment, should enable disabled people's views to shape service planning in the future.

It is of course essential that none of these avenues should prove to be a dead-end: every participation avenue/exercise must result in action and the outcome – even if interim – fed back to all who take part.

Individual empowerment

Many people lack the confidence, skills and experience to participate collectively or individually. In addition to supporting collective user action, localities must enable individual disabled people to express their opinions, make informed choices, and exercise their rights under law so that they can become self-assessors and self-advocates, and take up available opportunities (including the opportunity to participate in community care planning through a user group). Employing trained, experienced disabled people, and drawing on the expertise of disabled people's groups, to undertake empowerment work can be particularly effective.

- **In response to a Wirral Living Options Practice Team initiative, the social services training department invited the Living Options development worker to run a 'training needs analysis day' with the elected disabled representatives on the three Day Centres' Advisory Bodies. The aim was to build a programme of personal development training for disabled day centre users (each centre has six user members on its advisory body). It was acknowledged that day centre users had a limited understanding of the workings of the management setup and of the meaning of 'community care', and that they needed support in order to make an effective contribution to the advisory bodies. The value of the work is demonstrated by the interest of centre attenders in getting involved – 27 people stood for six places at the AGM of one centre. This work is recognised as just scratching the surface of need, and the aim is eventually to train all those who attend the centres.**

- In Maidstone, Wycombe and other Living Options localities consultants carried out personal development training with user group members to develop confidence and an understanding of disability issues and of planning systems.

- In Hereford, disabled people were encouraged to attend consultation meetings where independent facilitators led discussions about users' priorities. Also in Herefordshire, staff and volunteers with Herefordshire Lifestyles enable disabled people to live as they choose in the community by partnering them in considering their life plans.

- In Brent, the information, advice and outreach work carried out by the Asian People with Disabilities Alliance (APDA) has resulted in increased take-up of mainstream services by Asian disabled people. APDA, an organisation run by Asian disabled people, is also launching an advocacy service.

- In Hampshire, disabled people who live independently and manage their own care assistants under the county's Self Operated Care Scheme (SOCS) run courses on behalf of social services for other disabled people who are considering becoming SOCS users.

- In Solihull, a consultant is working with young disabled people to enable them to learn self-assessment skills and to act as their own case managers. Complementary work is being done with potential care managers. This pilot project, funded by the NHS Management Executive, aims to develop a model of case management which will be effective for both users and managers.

- In North Staffordshire, young disabled school leavers are involved in a programme to help them through the transition from school to independent adulthood. Young people were involved in the group setting up the service which included health, social services, careers office and the voluntary sector. Since launching the holistic Young Adult Service, they are routinely consulted about the service sessions and production of information materials.

Resourced user role

At a time of uncertain and restricted funding for community care, it is essential that user involvement is not dismissed as a 'luxury'. Legislation requires consultation on service planning with organisations representing users and carers, but more than 'consultation' is required. The impact on service development of disabled people employed or strongly organised in the voluntary sector should also be recognised, and is reflected in the examples cited in this report.

Disabled people's key role in achieving responsive services must be acknowledged by providing support, including financial support, for user participation. Commitment to user participation needs to be more than just lip service. Users must be confident that the 'system' values their contribution, and that they will see a change in practice.

Creation of posts to develop effective participation is essential. Newly forming groups require start-up costs – expertise and money – to enable them to become established and skilled. Secondments and offers of premises, equipment and other resources are helpful.

- **In Redbridge, joint finance provides £30,000 a year for three years to fund the Living Options development worker to facilitate user group development and user participation in community care planning. A three-year Living Options development worker post in Maidstone is also funded through joint finance.**

But effective input from disabled people also requires a long term commitment of time, work and resources. Mainstream funding is essential to enable disabled people to participate in service planning and to provide the advice and services required by authorities. Established groups require funds for core costs (for example, co-ordinator post, office and administration costs, training). Service agreements and contracts provide independence, clarity and security. The extra costs (transport, personal assistance, interpreters, sign language interpreters) of one-off pieces of work requested by authorities need to be funded additionally. Disabled people in most instances are helping local authorities to develop services without reimbursement for time or expenses.

- **In Hillingdon, the users' group, Disablement Association Hillingdon (DASH), which has been in existence for ten years, receives £72,000 from social services on a service agreement under which DASH provides information, training and consultation services. The Kingston Association of Disabled People (KADP), active for 24 years, will administer independent**

living funds totalling nearly £60,000 from April 1993 on behalf of social services. In addition, KADP receives £37,000 from social services for management and administration of the Association, as well as smaller amounts for provision of other services to the Borough.

The examples below show the kinds of services that can be provided for statutory authorities by adequately supported and resourced users' groups.

- **Culturally appropriate services for Asian disabled people and their carers and families are provided by the Asian People with Disabilities Alliance (APDA) in Brent. An Urban Programme grant provides four-year funding for a respite care project which aims to relieve isolation among Asian disabled people. A respite centre offers social activities in different languages, with food and music chosen by the users. Clients are referred by statutory and voluntary bodies such as the Brent Carers Consortium. APDA's work complements respite services offered by social services and Parkside Health Trust, who have helped APDA secure funding from a number of grant-making bodies. The project also offers a sitting/befriending scheme.**

- **A sexual counselling project, Obelisk, in Northampton has been formally established, with trained disabled counsellors. Training from Relate was paid through Health Promotion. The Northampton Council for the Disabled (a group managed by disabled people) is the referral point.**

- **CATCH-UP (Co-operative Action to Change and Hurry Up Progress), a disabled people's co-operative (awaiting Charity Commision approval) was formed by users of a social centre in Dyfed. In addition to involvement in service planning, training and quality action, CATCH-UP is running an information and advice service with the full support of Dyfed social services, and developing similar groups and user-run services in other parts of the county. The disabled information officer is working on a sheltered placement funded by social services and the Welsh Office. HELIOS I and Opportunities for Volunteers provide further funding. This service enables social services to fulfil obligations under Section 10 of the 1986 Disabled Persons Act; the health authority is involved through a joint working party.**

- **An advocacy service in Hillingdon, funded by City Parochial Foundation and run by DASH (Disablement Association Hillingdon), is provided by trained disabled advocates. Clients are recommended by social services. The service gives information and advice, and negotiates user complaints.**

Multi-agency partnerships

Bringing together in working teams representatives from all agencies that have an impact on disabled people's lives – housing, education and employment as well as health and social services – is essential to secure the 'seamless' service required for good community care. Face-to-face contact between service planners/providers and disabled people is also essential. Both are fundamental to the Living Options approach.

In the Living Options In Practice localities, multi-agency teams including disabled people were formed or strengthened, and established formal links with existing planning structures. Other localities have built similar systems in which disabled people have established strong representation and formed good working partnerships with professionals.

Many localities express concerns about the abandonment or marginalisation of partnership teams as new planning structures evolve. The experience and strengths of existing multi-agency teams should be 'exploited' by building them in to new planning systems. Multi-agency teams may be particularly important where user-run groups do not yet have a strong independent voice, and should be proactive in seeking involvement in new planning systems.

● **The Living Options Practice Team in Northallerton is a formal sub-group of the Joint Partnership Group. While disabled people are represented through the development worker on the Partnership Group, the Living Options Team has a brief to reach a wider group of disabled people. The Team includes the Living Options development worker and leaders of the three local Living Options user groups as well as social services, health and carer representatives.**

Partnerships across agencies can be cemented by jointly funding posts to further common aims.

● **In Hillingdon, a new community care co-ordinating post is funded by and accountable for a fixed term to social services, the health authority and the FHSA, to take a lead role in community care implementation, publicity and care management.**

Focus for action

Designation of senior-level posts with responsiblity for developing and co-ordinating disability services provides a vital catalyst and focus for action for disabled people and professionals. Employing disabled

people to fill key high-profile posts helps ensure provision of appropriate services while sending powerful messages to professionals and disabled people. Accountability across agencies is particularly important.

During the past few years the profile of physical and sensory disablity services has heightened in many localities. But positive developments are threatened by reorganisation and spending cuts and in some localities progress has ground to a halt. Jointly funded disability posts are being replaced by generic community care co-ordinators or care managers to assess and purchase individual services. Health-funded cross-agency disability co-ordination posts disappear as health authorities, which previously may have taken a lead role on disability, look to social services as lead agency. Some independent physical and sensory disability planning units are being merged with acute services or with services for elderly people in new planning systems. Morale is low among staff whose jobs are uncertain. Users have lost 'allies' within the system and feel left out of the loop.

Keeping disability issues high on the agenda and maintaining continuity of essential disability posts and staff is particularly important during this period of upheaval. There are many ways to create a focus for the development of responsive, co-ordinated disability services.

- **In Hampshire, a county level social services Disability Advisor supports the development of consumer groups, helps consolidate funding, identifies training needs and develops training programmes in communication, committee and advocacy skills.**

- **In Northampton, a health authority-funded Disability Co-ordinator takes a lead role across agencies. The co-ordinator of the Northampton Council for the Disabled (51 per cent disabled person managed) gives a strong voluntary sector lead. Joint finance has been agreed to employ two disabled development workers to build user participation across the county, using the consumer database and topic groups.**

- **Disability planning group chairs currently are filled by disabled people in East Devon (the Joint Disability Forum) and Northampton (the Living Options Group), and in some Living Options Practice Teams.**

- **The Living Options Practice Teams have employed development workers to facilitate user participation and develop user groups to work with the teams.**

The Living Options Partnership

This paper demonstrates ways in which planners, purchasers, providers and users, working in partnership, are developing strategies that give disabled people greater choice of and control over services. *Getting Results* provides examples of good practice from a number of localities, and suggests key factors necessary to achieve results. Despite this evidence, however, the overall picture of disability services emerging from this study, as community care comes into effect, is disappointing. Innovative work is stalled at the planning stage, and prospects for the future include diminished status of physical disability within community care strategies and real cuts in services.

'Business as usual' from April 1993 is unlikely to deliver the kinds of services that disabled people require. The challenge now is to find new ways to shift the balance from planning to development of services, drawing on the resource that disabled people and their organisations provide. The Living Options Partnership is commmitted to encouraging and supporting all those involved at a local, regional and national level in developing responsive commmunity care for disabled people.

This new phase of Living Options work will be responding to the challenge of community care and ensuring that service agencies and disabled people are at the forefront of shaping the planning, delivering and monitoring of quality services. The long term aim is to ensure that everyone is working towards increasing disabled people's control over their lives.

The Living Options Partnership will work towards:

- extending support to more localities which are establishing partnerships in service development;

- building a database and encouraging networking between people working in service development in disability services;

- promoting service development with Black disabled people;

- promoting links between purchasers and providers of user-controlled services;

- encouraging disabled people's involvement in policy and practice in community care.

For further information contact:

Living Options Partnership
126 Albert Street
London NW1 7NF
Tel. 071-267 6111
Fax. 071-267 6108

Living Options publications

Mail order
Post-free from:
Bournemouth English Book Centre
PO Box 1496, Poole, Dorset BH12 3YD
Tel. 0202-715555   Fax. 0202-715556

To personal callers
From the King's Fund Centre Bookshop,
126 Albert Street, London NW1 7NF.
Nearest tube station Camden Town.

Living Options Lottery	£6.00
A Framework For Action	£4.50
Tracking Success	£6.00
Achieving User Participation	£6.00
Getting Results	£6.00

For full references see page 12.

Contacts

An up-to-date contact for each locality or project cited in this paper can be obtained from the Living Options Partnership office.

27